IS THERE ROOM IN THE ALLEY FOR ANOTHER POET?

by Amy Lynn Hess

A Gypsy Daughter Chapbook

Copyright 2002 Amy Lynn Hess
Cover Image Copyright 2002 Erik Scherb

ISBN 0-9718068-0-2
ISBN 978-0-9718068-0-1

Dedication

The publishing of this book would not have been possible without significant contributions by the following chocolate chips on this great big cookie I call my life:

my uncle and godfather, Tim Polk
my sister, Renee Ann Hess
my beautiful cousin, Brenda Jayne Polk
my wondrous friend, Kia Kuresman
my muses, Mark, Matt, Matt, and Michael

and the biggest chocolate chip of all –
my mom, Traci Rumsey

Introduction

I have two friends who (without missing drags on their respective cigarettes) would always remind me to tell people that I am not a dramaturg, but am, in fact, a poet. Unknowing passers-by would often mistake me for a dramaturg in the days when I was getting my graduate degree in theatre history and criticism as a dramaturg. If I was too tired or mellow to correct this mistake by an unknowing passerby (or if the word "dramaturg" escaped my own lips) either one or both of them would correct the mistake for me. "You're a poet." And I would thank one or both of them. "Thank you."

So I am a poet. I think like a poet. I talk like a poet. I laugh like a poet. I cry like a poet. I write like a poet. And a passerby is one of those many people I have met on my cookie and they are part of my poetry. The places I have seen are my poetry and the pictures in my mind are my poetry and the memories I have shared and collected are my poetry. My feelings become my poetry. Sometimes all of that poetry is more like dramatic poesy, but I think that's just a residual symptom of my higher educational experience. It comes with being a poet who does dramaturgical work.

This first chapbook is dedicated to all of my chocolate chips, muses and poetry (especially that smoking section of my poetry) who call me, and first knew to call me a poet.

Amy Lynn Hess
July 24, 2001

TABLE OF CONTENTS

Through the Window of the Train Leaving Chicago 1

St. Christopher in the Sunshine Loki in the Rain .. 2

Lovebirds 3

The Man with the Big Crack Showing Responds to a Work Call Three Months Too Late or "Lou Loses an Eyebrow" 4

Before Bodyshame 5

It happened like a hole in my itchy woolen mitten. The cold found its way inside. 6

Jellyfish 7

Banging on Autumn's Door 8

Old Man in the Kitchen 9

Bull Rider 10

Reflection on My Lack of Political Efficacy 11

Rejecting the Phallic Microchip or "Harmony" ... 12

Grit in My Teeth From 13

He tasted like beer and poetry, pool and the barhaze of Wednesday night. 14

I came to your window 15

Cinquains for March 2001 16

Mark's Definition of Poetry 17

Words 20

Through the Window of the Train Leaving Chicago

the view was deadtired stale
and drenched in beatbrown silence

except for where angrybored somebodies had
spraypainted tags in
firehydrant red and
toybox blue on
boardedup ghostridden warehouses
crackhouses
houses

and except for where two miniature coats
one in
firehydrant red and
one in
toybox blue
played hopscotch in a faroff streetscape alongside a
tan and rustcolored 1978 Impala with four
flat tires

-July 15, 2001-

St. Christopher in the Sunshine Loki in the Rain

One handed in a red car she sped into the city,
and the city greeted her through the open window
with the smell of exhaust
and the sting of hard rain on her face and left arm
as she stretched and twisted her left arm
through said open window
in a preventative attempt to keep a wild wiper
from jumping ship onto I-75.

-April 18, 2001-

LOVEBIRDS

the lovebirds thought they were safe
i suppose
taking their roll in the green spring grass
flapflopping this way and that
until splat
they bouncefloundered off the median right onto 285
and became one with each other
the concrete and a Uniroyal

-May 21, 2001-

The Man with the Big Crack Showing Responds to a Work Call Three Months Too Late or "Lou Loses an Eyebrow"

"so yous girls's stove's leaking gas,"
grunts maintenance man,
raising an eyebrow sardonically before he lights the match

"I don't smell nuttin'"
peering into the burner
as he lights the match
the dilapidated stove torching the ass

and it feel real good when I laugh
and laugh
and laugh

Before Bodyshame

age 10
Sunday sunlight sticky on my tan skin
nothing but naked under my thin nightgown
singing loud
taking my time
throwing stones and a little kid shadow
across the bumpy gravel
in my mom's ka-thunking sandals
down the edge of the dirt driveway to the paperbox
for the funnies
with wet grass stuck to my soft unshaven legs

IT HAPPENED LIKE A HOLE IN MY ITCHY WOOLEN MITTEN.
THE COLD FOUND ITS WAY INSIDE.

and just like closing the window after a storm
it's too late to do anything
but pry the wet bedsheets from the wall
and wait for the mattress
and soggy feather pillow to dry
so if you try to rest here now
you'll succeed only in numbing your warm pink check
against my frosty blue existence.

Jellyfish

there were 2 washed-up jellyfish
shining in the sun
on the beach at the shore

a cruel wave swept in
and took back the jellyfish on the right
but the other lay abandoned in the cold, damp sand
and siltsalty foam stuck to her still body

but I dared played God
and I lifted the limpdead jellyfish back into the ocean
so she could float away

-October 1, 2001-

Banging on Autumn's Door

Old man Winter came stumbling home
(a veritable deranged Santa
with three missing front teeth
delirium tremens
musty woolen trousers
and cigar breath)
heaving himself up like a bowl of lead-laced jelly
past the frozen pumpkin,
up the chipped and icy cement steps
fumblin' for his keys
and grumblin' 'bout the price of sleighs.

Old Man in the Kitchen

picked up the dishcloth
wiped his coffee cup, ignored the stains
and stared with his mustache crooked in a look of
disgust
at the mashed fly parts
ground into the red and white and red squares

rinsed out the dishcloth with cold water
wiped his cereal bowl, ignore the chip
and smiled toothlessly out the window with a look of
satisfaction
at his squeaky clean dishes
stacked to dry in the grimy yellow rack

-March 2001-

Bull Rider

The cowboy
ambles
(a lit
tle
stiff-sore)
into the chiro
practor's
off
ice
(slow-like)
Heavy
by the
weight
of his (new)
sil
ver
buck
le.

Reflection on My Lack of Political Efficacy

the gerontocracy deems us generation x
the so-called apathetic generation
united in these states of confusion,
and somewhere between what we have not done
and what we have left

we ain't got the money, honey
they ain't got the time

hypocritical kiddie porno watching
white Anglo Saxon Protestant Male
deals dope from the tinted windows of his foreign car
speaks condemnation of welfare thieving alien
hoodlum ethnicities
goes home hits his wife
rapes his daughter
and kicks the damn dog

he's on a talkshow
and the animal rights people get him voted out of
office

animal abusing slimeball

little brother waves at the neighbors
(hide the fine china, Irene)
he yells, "I am not a crook!"
hippie ass burger flippin' no good no clue liberal kid
probably doesn't know catsup is a vegetable.

Rejecting the Phallic Microchip or "Harmony"

Censor what you say today
in a world full of peeping prodding toms
who will question your singing harmony and back-up
both at the same time

Or whether you will wither
when the wind gets too cold.

Being smart enough to know the difference
between one blue line or two
is what separates me from you
in my endeavor to protect my ovum
from the mass culture vacuum;
the phosphorescent consumer interior.

Dandies weren't born this way
but style is here to stay.
So, sing yuppie class prisoners.
Sing with middle class refugees
an ode to Capitalism, sex and violence
on the grassy knoll.

Maybe when They lean the rules
a matriarch will order wine
and there we'll sit and talk and dine
romantically of kings and fools.

"Man is no longer noble," says Joseph Wood Krutch.

Grit in My Teeth From

dangling down
head first
arms wedged one behind my back
one beneath my belly
in the bottleneck of Beelzebub's hourglass eggtimer

I taste the dry sand slide by
rubbing my stickout parts
pink raw

HE TASTED LIKE BEER AND POETRY, POOL AND THE
BARHAZE OF WEDNESDAY NIGHT.

when I remembertaste the man on my lips
with my tongue and memory
I wonder why he wants me to forgive
all the parts that make him

I CAME TO YOUR WINDOW

like you asked me to
stood in the rain and you slept
with a book in your hand with the light on
slept

I was soaked drunk outside
may as well've been naked
so I started down the hill to go back to the bar
where it was warm and noisy
but decided to come back by the time I got to the
alley

lifted my hand to knock
rolled over as you slept
dropped your book and the light went out

-March 2001-

Cinquains for March 2001

Wasteful
to only be
thinking of his chin. How
would my head fit in the crook of
his arm?

The path
that connects his
heart to his soul to blue
eyes is often used. Well worn and
beaten.

Now, if
he doesn't show
up in my dreams or at
least wander to my door I'll be
waiting.

Mark's Definition of Poetry

Mark Alan Vanfossen, July 15, 2001-

I told my mother – I spent last week in Virginia, in the mountains, and withdrawn – that poetry is like a hurricane that blows down trees; it turns over cars and raises fish to do dramatic things. Let your poetry find you, sweetheart, or you will find insanity holding out its broken arm like a hobo, but not he hobo generally, rather his toothpick or maybe just a bit of toothpick sticking out of the corner of a hungry grin. That's where I find my poetry.

I'm going to go stare at beautiful girls and write some poetry and slow dance with the sun now. I hope this finds you smiling.

Mark Alan Vanfossen, July 16, 2001-

What exactly WAS my definition of poetry? It changes so rapidly that I seldom can keep up with it. Perhaps that means that the new definition of my poetry is something like "Poetry is like run children running through a yard with a stolen can, waving it around like a magic wand – changing trees into dragons, bees into castles – while grandfather sits on the front porch yelling 'where the hell is your damn mother, damn it, come back here... damn it... Keep that dad-blasted dragon outta' my corn!!!'" And then time freezes, the wind crystallizes, and forever we are all captured – the children, grandpa, and me... – the notebook closes like a coffin, we move on to the next place... Perhaps that is poetry to me today.

May your day be changed into crystal castles and trees made of honey.

Note to Reader: Grandpa actually yells, "Hey! You in the Corn!" That's how the mythological horse with the corn cob sticking out of his ear became dubbed the "unicorn."

-Amy

Second Note to Reader: See, I don't believe that, because it was really grandpa with the corn sticking out of his ear – he's getting gold, bless his heart – that's why he didn't see the poetry... er, children, stealing his cane...

-Mark

Words

Catsup – fed to me when I was in grade school as a vegetable because it's cheaper than real vegetables

Chocolate chips – gifts I find in my life (mostly people)

Cinquain – a poetic structure based on syllable count

Cookie – my life

Dandy – one too concerned with appearance, a fop

Delirium tremens – drunken shakes accompanied by tracers and fuzzy teeth

Dramaturg – a person who tries to learn and teach something or everything about a play to someone or everyone (including cast, crew, director, writer, and audience) throughout the production process

Efficacy – belief in one's ability to effect change

Gerontocracy – old bureaucrats who run the country

Integritis – one who speaks and theorizes with great integrity of philosophy

Loki – mythological god of mischief

Muse – an inspiration

Noble – having moral and ethical character

Other people who've made a big difference in my life – Jason(s), Chris(s), Shawn, Matt(s), Lori, Heather, Becky, Jo, Kathy, Jill, Todd, Rachel, Ryan, Addae, Erik, Kyle, and Sue

Phosphorescent – a type of greenish, non-natural glow

Sardonic – wry and condescendingly cynical

Silver buckle – prize won and often worn by bull riders, it has been adopted by the fashion industry this year making many, cheap, tin versions available in malls across America

Surreptitiously – done with "sneak"

Vanfossen, Fick, Smith, and Kennedy – last names, respectively, of the muses mentioned in this book

Veritable – bona fide

285 – the evil and foul Atlanta loop, related to I-75 and GA 400

www.ingramcontent.com/pod-product-compliance
Lightning Source LLC
Chambersburg PA
CBHW061349040426
42444CB00011B/3163